EXECUTIVE EDITORS
Sarah Galbraith, Alan Doan,
Jenny Doan, David Mifsud

MANAGING EDITOR
Natalie Earnheart

CREATIVE DIRECTOR
Christine Ricks

PHOTOGRAPHERS
Mike Brunner, Lauren Dorton

VIDEOGRAPHER
Jake Doan

TECHNICAL WRITER
Edie McGinnis

TECHNICAL EDITOR
Denise Lane

PATTERN LAYOUT DESIGN
Ally Simmons

PROJECT DESIGN TEAM
Natalie Earnheart, Jenny Doan,
Sarah Galbraith

AUTHOR OF QUILT TALES
Nichole Spravzoff

CONTRIBUTING COPYWRITERS
Jenny Doan, Natalie Earnheart, Christine Ricks,
Katie Mifsud, Camille Maddox, Nichole Spravzoff,
Edie McGinnis

COPY EDITOR
Nichole Spravzoff

CONTRIBUTING PIECERS
Jenny Doan, Natalie Earnheart, Carol Henderson,
Denise Lane, Janice Richardson

CONTRIBUTING QUILTERS
Jamey Stone-Manager, Sarah Richardson - Training
Specialist, Becky Bowen - Quilting Customer
Service, Linda Frump - Quilt Check-In Specialist,
Nikki LaPiana-Quilting Coordinator, Sandy Moss
- Backing Specialist, Angela Wilson,Linda Frump,
Debbie Elder, Betty Bates, Karla Zinkand, Jan Meek,
Chelsea White, Debbie Allen, Charlene Ensz, Jamee
Gilgour, Stephanie Weaver, Jennifer Dowling,
Christine Atteberry - Pulley, Natalie Loucks, Dennis
Voss, Kara Snow - Night Assist Manager, Devin
Ragle, Rachael Joyce, Bruce Van Iperen, Francesca
Flemming, Aaron Crawford, Ethan Lucas, Lyndia
Lovell, Cyera Cottrill, Salena Smiley, Deborah
Warner

BINDING SPECIALISTS
Elizabeth Hostetler, Deloris Burnett, Bernice Kelly

PRINTING COORDINATOR
Rob Stoebener

PRINTING SERVICES
Walsworth Print Group
803 South Missouri
Marceline, MO 64658

CONTACT US
Missouri Star Quilt Company
114 N Davis
Hamilton, Mo. 64644
888-571-1122
info@missouriquiltco.com

content

Oops! Sometimes we make mistakes.
To find corrections to every issue of Block
go to: **www.msqc.co/corrections**

hello
from MSQC

At the beginning of a fresh, new year, I feel hopeful about all the good things that can happen in just the space of 365 days. Each day is a new beginning and I am amazed at how much change can take place over a year. I've barely had time to sit down and consider all the wonderful things that have happened last year and now we're well into 2017.

A lot of us make goals during this time of year and these goals might include things like finishing up a few sewing projects that may have piled up over the years or tackling a disorganized sewing room. Although it can be overwhelming to think about all those projects at once, when we work on the small things, bit by bit, somehow the larger things take care of themselves.

Let this be the beginning of a great year. I hope this issue of Block leaves you feeling motivated to make something new and finish up those pesky WIPs. I know you can do it! So, take heart, dear quilters. I believe in you and all the marvelous things you can do. Keep in mind that handmade can't be rushed and these processes take time. And, most importantly, don't forget to have fun while you're at it!

JENNY DOAN
MISSOURI STAR QUILT CO

4

TRY OUR APP

It's easy to keep up on every issue of BLOCK magazine. Access it from all your devices. And when you subscribe to BLOCK, it's free with your subscription!

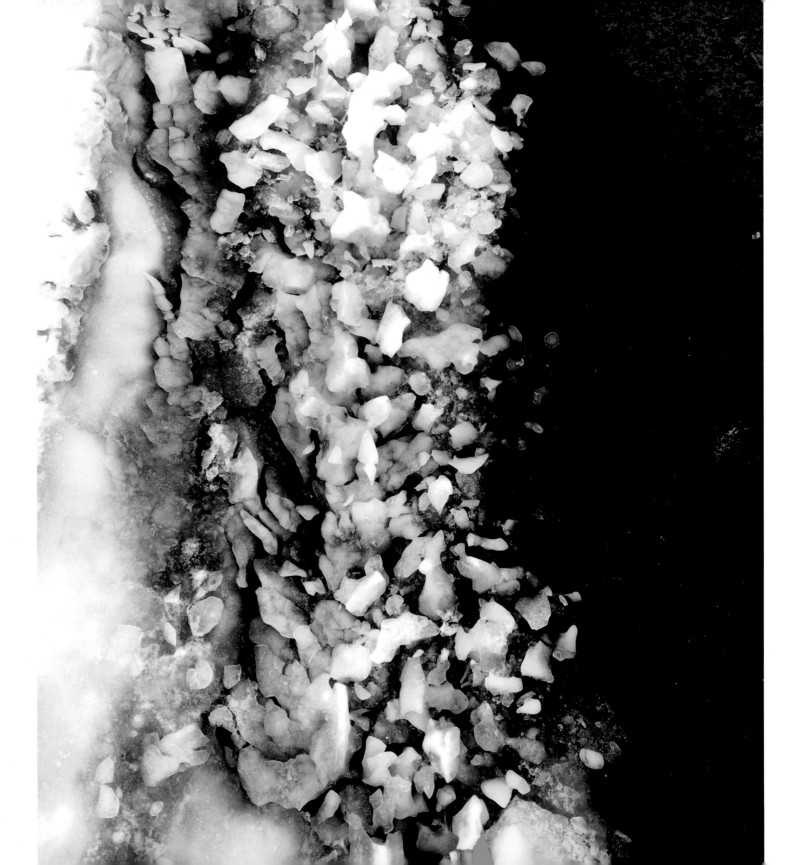

new year,
new ideas

How do you feel about the new year? Does it bring with it anxiety and doubt or a fresh perspective and newfound creativity? For me it's a mixture of both. I feel an inordinate amount of pressure to come up with new goals and new ideas, but when I take away the pressure and pause for a minute, I find the process can be quite rewarding and satisfying.

I don't like to set "goals." I will either change my habits or life will change what I thought I needed into something else. It also leaves me feeling inadequate at times, and we don't need that now, do we? Instead, I like to make lists of things I want to accomplish, with some fun thrown in there as well—those things always get accomplished! That way, when I need it, I have something to look forward to when I need to focus. Plus, it always feels good to cross something off the list.

Quilting works the same way for me. Start out this year by making a list of all the ideas you want to learn, explore, or make, and then start crossing them off the list! You'll be pleased at how good it feels. It's all about enjoying the journey. Happy travels!

CHRISTINE RICKS
MSQC Creative Director, BLOCK MAGAZINE

PRINTS

FBY43690 Hey Dot - Sketched White
by Zen Chic for Moda Fabrics
SKU: 1604 11

FBY46389 Vine - Plaid Blue by The Henry Ford
Archive for Windham Fabrics SKU: 42290-4

FBY45448 House of Hoppington - Frolic Blueberry
by Violet Craft for Michael Miller
SKU: DC7303-BREE-D

FBY31469 Touch of Grey - Triangles Smoke by
Whistler Studios for Windham Fabrics
SKU: 41198G-5

FBY35303 Neighborhood - Words Grey
by Alyson Beaton for Windham Fabrics
SKU: 41283-4

FBY24727 Parisian - Diamond Black
by Chelsea Anderson for Riley Blake
SKU: C4633-BLACK

SOLIDS

FBY1168 Bella Solids - White Bleached
by Moda Fabrics
SKU: 9900 98

FBY3206 Bella Solids - Home Town Sky
by Moda Fabrics
SKU: 9900 177

FBY12195 Bella Solids - Indigo
by Moda Fabrics
SKU: 9900 218

FBY42796 Bella Solids - Taupe
by Moda Fabrics
SKU: 9900 310

FBY12170 Bella Solids - Etchings Slate
by Moda Fabrics
SKU: 9900 170

FBY1059 Bella Solids Black
by Moda Fabrics
SKU: 9900 99

broken
orange
peel

Years ago, a young friend of mine set a very simple New Year's resolution, "Go on a date before the end of the year." Little did he know that this resolution would change his life forever. If you knew that one small change would make your life better, how hard would you work to reach that goal? How brave could you be? Well, this young man was about to find out.

Nathan was a brilliant mathematician, but despite his talents, he lacked confidence with the opposite sex, and in all his 22 years, he had never been kissed or even had a girlfriend. So, he set a goal for himself, to go on his very first date.

He started out the year hopeful, but as time marched on and the girls seemed oblivious, the goal of his first date remained unfulfilled. When college let out for spring break, Nathan's family made plans to meet relatives for a hike through the deserts of central Utah. The day before the outing, Nathan received a voice mail from his aunt, a professor at the local university.

She enthusiastically said, "Hi Nathan! Excited to see you tomorrow! Just wanted to let you know that I've invited one

8

For the tutorial and everything need you to make this quilt visit:
www.msqc.co/blockwinter17

of my favorite students to join us on the hike. I promised you'd show her around. I know you two will hit it off!"

Nathan felt his stomach tighten into a knot. Was this a date? It sounded like a date! Was he actually about to embark on his very first date in the presence of siblings, cousins, and grandparents? Then his thoughts turned from anticipation to anxiety. What a nightmare!

After a restless night, Nathan got up early to prepare for the day. He took extra care to neatly style his hair and choose a shirt that was clean and pressed. As a self-proclaimed nerd, he'd never bothered much with looking cool, but today was different. He examined his reflection in the mirror with a little nagging self-doubt, smiled anyway, then climbed into the family van for the long ride to the trailhead.

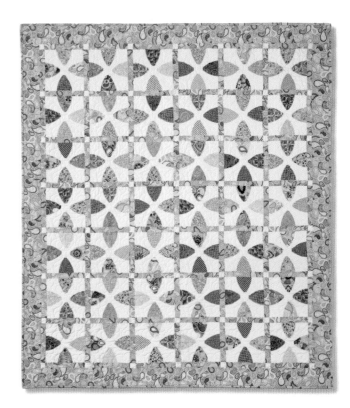

The moment Nathan locked eyes with Tricia, however, his anxiety melted away. Tricia was beautiful, friendly, and intelligent. Nathan was surprised to discover just how easily they fell into familiar conversation. As they hiked together, everyone else seemed to fade away.

Seventeen years have passed since Nathan's private vow to go on a date, and I think he (and Tricia) would agree, that his resolution was met with spectacular success. Two weeks before the year's end, on a beautiful snowy day, Nathan and Tricia were married and began their journey toward happily ever after.

Dreams do come true, but not by magic. May we all have the courage, and the gumption, to really chase those dreams, one simple goal at a time!

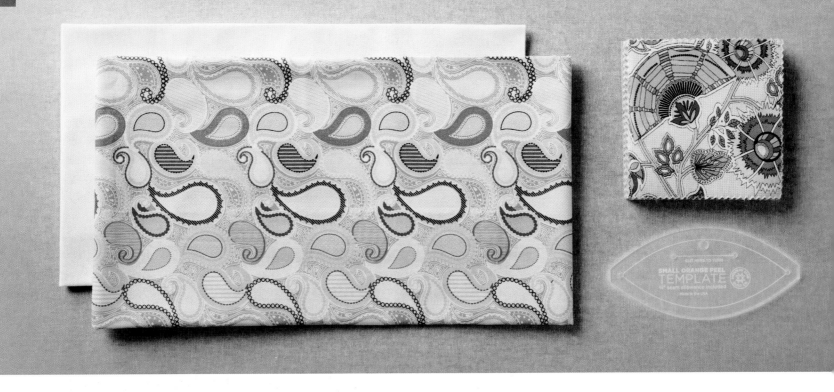

materials

makes a 59" X 67½" quilt

QUILT TOP
2 packages 5" print squares
2¼ yards background fabric

OUTER BORDER
1¾ yards – includes fabric for
  sashing strips

BINDING
¾ yard

BACKING
3¾ yards – horizontal seam(s)

ADDITIONAL SUPPLIES
Glue Stick
Small Orange Peel Template

SAMPLE QUILT
Sundance by Sue Daley for
Riley Blake

1 cut

From the background fabric, cut:

- (9) 8" strips across the width of
  the fabric. Subcut 8 strips into
  (5) 8" squares for a **total of 40
  squares**. Cut (2) 8" squares from
  the remaining strip. You should now
  have (42) 8" squares.

From the remaining 8" x 24"
background strip, cut:

- (4) 1½" x 24" strips – Subcut each of
  the strips into (16) 1½" squares. You
  need a total of (56) 1½" squares. Set
  these squares aside to use as
  cornerstones in the sashing.

From the outer border fabric, cut:

- (20) 1½" strips across the width of the
  fabric. Subcut each strip into (5) 1½" x
  8" rectangles. You need a **total
  of 97 rectangles.** Set the
  rectangles aside to use as sashing. We
  will cut the remaining fabric when we
  make the borders, so set it aside for
  the moment.

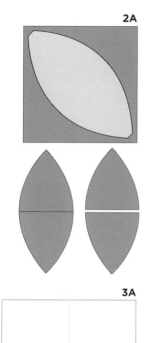
2A

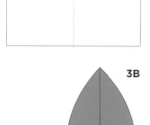
3A

3B

3C

4A

5A

2 appliqué pieces

Place the Small Orange Peel Template on each 5″ print square on the diagonal and cut around the shape using your rotary cutter. Cut 84. Fold each orange peel in half and press a crease on the fold. Cut each oval in half on the crease. You need a **total of 168 halves** for the blocks. **2A**

3 appliqué

Fold a 8″ background square in half vertically and horizontally. Pinch the folds so the fabric creases on the very edges. **3A**

Fold each appliqué piece in half horizontally. Pinch the fold to mark the crease in place. **3B**

Using the glue stick, dab a few spots of glue on the reverse side of the appliqué piece. Align the crease of the appliqué piece with the crease that you pinched into the background piece. Smooth the half-orange peel in place and stitch it down using a blanket stitch. Repeat for 3 half-orange peel pieces to complete the block.

Make 42 blocks. 3C

Block Size: 7½″ Finished

4 lay out blocks

Lay out the blocks in rows with each row having **6 blocks**. You need to lay out **7 rows.**

When you are satisfied with the arrangement, begin sewing the blocks and sashing into rows. Begin and end each row with a sashing rectangle and add an 8″ x 1½″ sashing rectangle between each block. **4A**

5 make sashing rows

Sew a 1½″ background square to a 1½″ x 8″ print sashing rectangle. Repeat until you have a sashing row consisting of (7) 1½″ background squares and 6 print sashing rectangles. **Make 8 rows. 5A**

6 arrange and sew

Lay out the quilt top. The top row should be a sashing row, the second row, sashed blocks. Continue to alternate the two rows until you have sewn all the rows together, ending with a row of sashing. See the diagram on pg. 15.

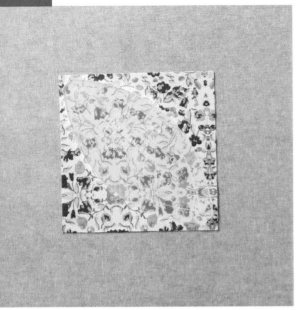

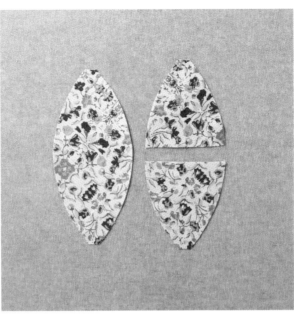

1 Place the small Orange Peel Template on each 5″ print square. Cut around the shape using a rotary cutter.

2 Fold each orange peel shape in half, then cut on the fold line.

3 Appliqué 4 half-orange peel pieces to an 8″ background square.

4 Add a 1½″ x 8″ sashing rectangle between each block as the rows are sewn together. Between each row, add a sashing row made of 1½″ cornerstones and 1½″ x 8″ sashing rectangles.

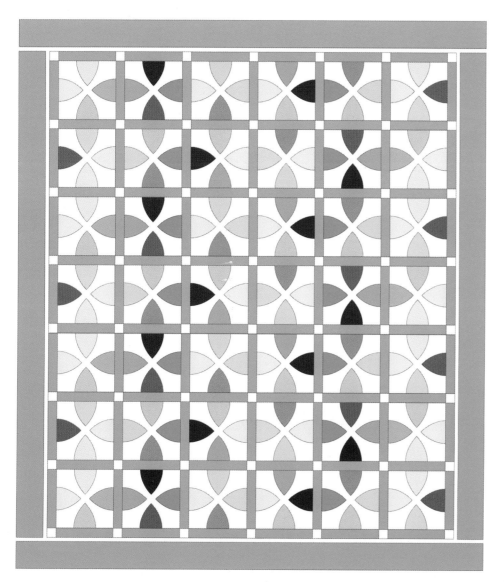

7 border

Cut (7) 4″ strips across the width of the fabric. Sew the strips together end-to-end to make one long strip. Trim the borders from this strip.

Refer to Borders (pg. 103) in the Construction Basics to measure and cut the outer borders. The strips are approximately 61″ for the sides and approximately 59½″ for the top and bottom.

8 quilt and bind

Layer the quilt with batting and backing and quilt. After the quilting is complete, square up the quilt and trim away all excess batting and backing. Add binding to complete the quilt. See Construction Basics (pg. 104) for binding instructions.

For the tutorial and everything you need to make this quilt visit:
www.msqc.co/blockwinter17

checkered dresden

One winter day, Ron invited me on a date to go ice skating. There was an outdoor rink in the next town over and neither of us had been ice skating before, but we were pretty good on roller skates. We figured, how hard could it be?

We bundled up in warm clothing and headed to the ice skating rink where we traded our shoes for skates. After tying the laces tight, looping the long strands around my ankles, I took a deep breath and shuffled from the bench to the edge of the rink on wobbly legs. *So far, so good,* I told myself. Then, with extreme care, I ventured out onto the ice. I quickly realized that I was in way over my head.

Clinging to the wall for dear life, I contemplated my next move. Meanwhile, Ron had stepped around me and sailed off with the greatest of ease. I watched in disbelief as he glided effortlessly around the perimeter of the rink. As he came back around the circle, he called out, "Just try it! Let go of the wall!"

So I did. I let go. For a fraction of a second, it was just me and the ice. Then, almost immediately, I lost control. My legs slid out and my ankles were wrenched at a dangerous angle. Frantically, I reached out for the wall. Once steady, I began to baby-step my way around the rink, both hands holding fast to that wall. I was so focused, I almost didn't notice Ron skate back over to me. He slid up, turned his blades sideways, and came to a stop with a dramatic spray of ice.

Snuggling in behind me, he whispered, "Come on, I will help you." Much to my amazement, he turned around and began to skate backwards. Stretching out his hands to me, he begged me to let go of the wall. It was a romantic gesture, but I was unconvinced. Just then, we came upon an opening in the

wall and, as quickly as I could, I ducked out and made a teetering beeline back to the safety of the bench.

I took off those wretched skates and spent the rest of the evening admiring my first-time-skating husband from a distance as he put everyone else to shame with his incredible skill. He was a natural, and just as easily as he could roller skate, he could ice skate. It didn't work that way for me, and I have yet to return to the ice skating rink. I suppose we all have different talents in life. Of course, it's always fun to try something new, but the next time Ron heads to the rink, I think I'll stay home and quilt!

materials

makes a 79½" X 79½" quilt

QUILT TOP
1 roll of 2½" strips
5¾ yards background fabric

OUTER BORDER
2 yards print – includes yardage to
   make circles for block centers

BINDING
¾ yard

BACKING
7½ yards – vertical seam(s)

ADDITIONAL SUPPLIES
MSQC Dresden Plate Template
½ yard lightweight fusible
   interfacing – We used Heat N Bond
   Feather Lite

SAMPLE QUILT
Artisan Batiks Daisy's Garden 3 by Lunn
Studios for Robert Kaufman

1 cut

From the background fabric, cut:

- (9) 22" strips across the width of the
  fabric – Cut (1) 22" square from each
  strip. Set the rest of the fabric aside
  for another project.

From the border fabric, cut:

- (1) 4¼" strip across the width of the
  fabric – subcut the strip into 4¼"
  squares for a total of 9 squares. Set
  aside for the moment.

2 make strip sets

Sew (4) 2½" strips together to make one
strip set. **Make 10.**

3 cut

From each strip set, cut 18 blades using
the MSQC Dresden Plate template. Align
the **8½"** mark on the template with the
top of the strip set. As you cut, flip the
template 180 degrees to get more pieces
per strip. You need a **total of 180 blades.**
3A

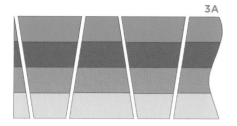

3A

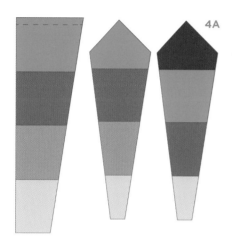

4A

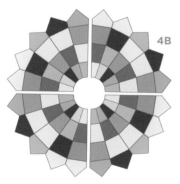

4B

5A

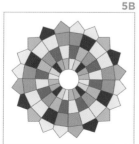

5B

4 sew

Fold each blade in half lengthwise with right sides facing and stitch across the top. Turn each blade right side out and press. **4A**

Sew 20 blades together into a circle. If it's easier for you to handle, make the circle in 4 sections of 5 blades each, then sew the sections together to complete the circle. **Make 9 circles. 4B**

5 appliqué

Fold a background square in half vertically and again horizontally. Lightly press the creases in place. **5A**

Fold the Dresden Circles in half along the seam lines vertically and horizontally. Align the seams with the creases in the background fabric and pin in place. Appliqué the circle in place using a small blanket stitch. **Make 9. 5B**

5C

Refer to the template for the 4" circle on page 23 and trace 9 circles onto the fusible interfacing.

Place a fusible interfacing circle onto a 4¼" square with right sides facing. (The bumpy side of the interfacing will face the right side of the fabric.) Sew ¼" inside of the drawn circle, then trim on the drawn line. Cut a slit in the fusible, and turn the circle right side out, smoothing the edges as you turn so the piece will lie flat. Press the circle to the center of the Dresden Plate. Using a blanket stitch, sew the circle in place. Repeat for the remaining blocks. **5C**

Block Size: 21½" Finished

6 arrange in rows

Arrange the blocks in **3 rows** with each row having **3 blocks.** Once you are happy with the arrangement, sew the blocks together. Press the seam allowances of the odd numbered rows toward the right and the even numbered row toward the left to make the seams nest. Sew the rows together.

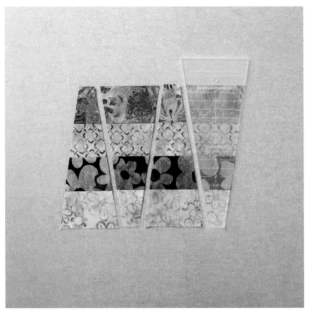

1 Align the 8½″ mark on the MSQC Dresden Plate Template on the top of a strip set. Flip the template 180° with each cut to make the most of the fabric.

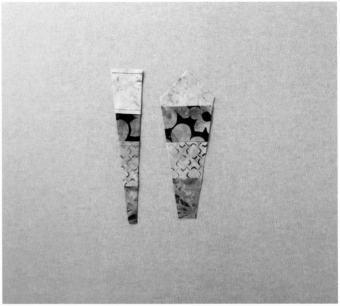

2 Fold each blade in half with right sides facing and sew across the top. Turn the piece right side out.

3 After sewing and trimming the fusible interfacing to the piece being used for the center of the Dresden Plate, cut a slit in the interfacing and turn right side out.

4 Press the circle to the center of the Dresden Plate and appliqué in place using a blanket stitch.

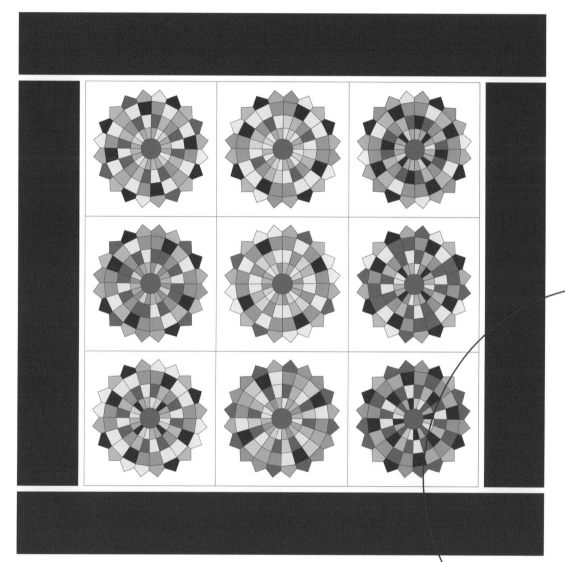

7 border

Cut (8) 8" strips across the width of the fabric. Sew the strips together end-to-end to make one long strip. Trim the borders from this strip.

Refer to Borders (pg. 103) in the Construction Basics to measure and cut the outer borders. The strips are approximately 65" for the sides and approximately 80" for the top and bottom.

8 quilt and bind

Layer the quilt with batting and backing and quilt. After the quilting is complete, square up the quilt and trim away all excess batting and backing. Add binding to complete the quilt. See Construction Basics (pg. 104) for binding instructions.

4" circle

For the tutorial and everything you need to make this quilt visit:
www.msqc.co/blockwinter17

disappearing
pinwheel
arrows

It's a bird! It's a plane! No, it's a UFO! In the quilting world, we have a lot of words for projects we've begun and left unfinished. Some call them "UFOs" (unfinished objects), but I actually prefer to call them "WIPs" (works in progress), because a work in progress sounds like it could be finished at any moment! It's just a more positive way of looking at things, I suppose. Don't worry, I won't nag you about them. I've got my own fair share of WIPs. But I do have some advice that helps me keep going when the projects start piling up.

So, here's the first thing to think about. If something's out of sight, it's out of mind. Pull out your projects and put them right where you can see them. That way, when a wave of inspiration strikes you, it's easy to get to work right away. Clear storage bins help with this, as well as open shelves. Stack up your beautiful stash where you can see it and go ahead and use it. It's begging to be made into something awesome!

My second hint is to be honest with yourself. If you truly dislike a project, give it away to a quilt guild so they can make it into a donation quilt, or have the courage to go off-pattern and make it into something totally new. Your time is valuable, so spend it on what matters. It's okay to part with those things that don't bring you joy.

Third, just relax and get a pizza. I'm serious! Go out and grab a slice and while you're at it, pick up a few clean, empty pizza boxes and use them to organize your WIPs. It might sound a little crazy, but it works! I take my projects and separate them into the boxes. They stack nice and flat and have plenty of room inside. As I put materials into the pizza boxes, I make a list of everything I need to finish that project, that way I am able to judge the time needed to complete the project.

Sometimes my grandkids joke that the Teenage Mutant Ninja Turtles must visit my sewing room with all the pizza boxes in there!

Finally, set aside a WIP sewing time. As you chip away throughout the year, you'll notice that your burden will be considerably lighter. A few minutes a day can make all the difference! The same is true for any goal.

When all's said and done, I'm sure it won't matter if a couple projects are left for the next generation, but give yourself the gift of time and allow for a window of creativity to open up in your life. Even if you don't produce much, the time you spent making will give you much needed tranquility in a world that barely stops to take a breath.

26

materials

makes an 81" X 92" quilt

QUILT TOP
1 package 10" print squares
1 package of 10" background
  squares

INNER BORDER
¾ yard

OUTER BORDER
1¾ yards

BINDING
¾ yard

BACKING
7½ yards – horizontal seam(s)

SAMPLE QUILT
Jubilee by Melody Miller for
Cotton + Steel

1 make half-square triangles

Layer a 10" print square with a 10" background square with right sides facing. Sew all the way around the outside edge using a ¼" seam allowance. Cut the sewn squares from corner to corner twice on the diagonal. Open and press the seam allowance toward the darker fabric. Each set will yield 4 half-square triangles. You need a **total of 168** half-square triangles or 42 sets. Trim each half-square triangle to 6½". **1A**

Sew 4 half-square triangles together to make a pinwheel. **1B**

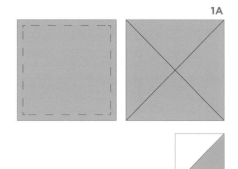

Measure your sewn block. Divide your measurement by 3 so you can cut your block into thirds. It should be about 4⅛". Divide that number in half if you would like to use the center seam as a

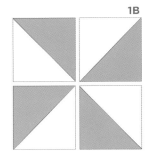

1B

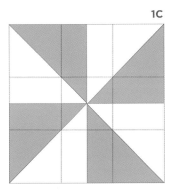

1C

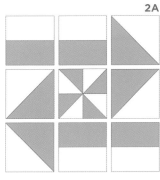

2A

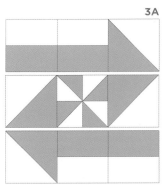

3A

guide. If you're using the center seam, measure out $2\frac{1}{16}$" inches (or half of your measurement) and cut on either side of the center seam horizontally and vertically. **1C**

2 trading places

The center pinwheel does not move. Turn the upper right and lower left half-square triangles one-fourth turn, the print triangle will point toward the center pinwheel. Move the two remaining half-square triangles to the center row. Turn them so the print triangles form an arrow point with the corner half-square triangles. Align (2) 2-patch pieces end-to-end to form an arrow shaft in the first and third rows of the block. **2A**

3 sew

You now have the pieces that make up 3 rows of a 9-patch block. Sew the pieces into rows as shown, then sew the rows together to complete the block. **Make 42 blocks. 3A**

Block Size: 11" Finished

4 arrange in rows

Arrange the blocks into rows with each row having **6 blocks** across. Notice that every other block is turned, altering the direction the arrows point. **Make 7 rows.** When you are happy with the way the quilt is laid out, sew the blocks together. Press the odd numbered rows toward the left and the even numbered rows toward the right. This way the seams will nest and make the corners easier to match.

Sew the rows together.

5 inner border

Cut (8) 2½" strips across the width of the fabric. Sew the strips together end-to-end to make one long strip. Trim the borders from this strip.

Refer to Borders (pg. 103) in the Construction Basics to measure and cut the inner borders. The strips are approximately 77½" for the sides and approximately 70½" for the top and bottom.

6 outer border

Cut (9) 6" strips across the width of the fabric. Sew the strips together end-to-end to make one long strip. Trim the borders from this strip.

Refer to Borders (pg. 103) in the Construction Basics to measure and cut the outer borders. The strips are approximately 81½" for the sides and approximately 81½" for the top and bottom.

7 quilt and bind

Layer the quilt with batting and backing and quilt. After the quilting is complete, square up the quilt and trim away all excess batting and backing. Add binding to complete the quilt. See Construction Basics (pg. 104) for binding instructions.

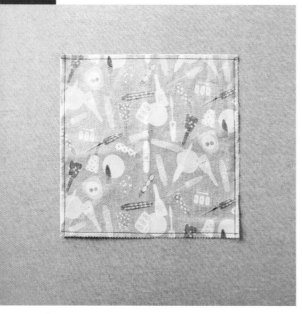

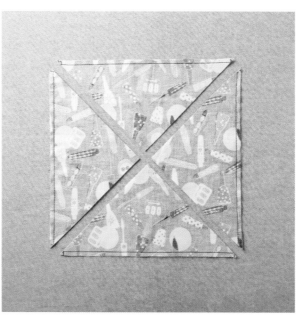

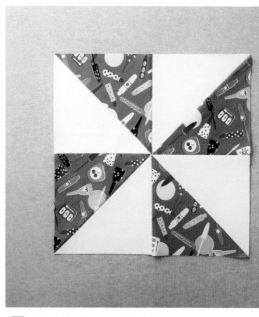

1 Layer a print 10″ square with a background 10″ square with right sides facing. Sew all the way around the perimeter using a ¼″ seam allowance.

2 Cut the sewn squares from corner to corner twice on the diagonal.

3 Sew 4 half-square triangles together to form a pinwheel.

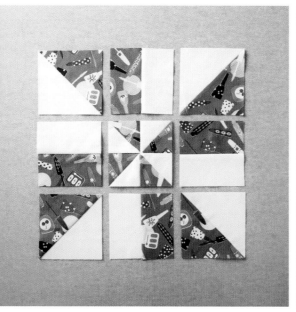

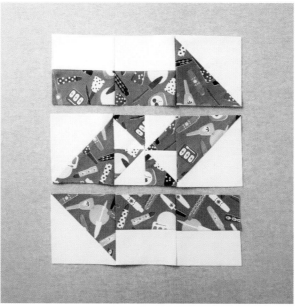

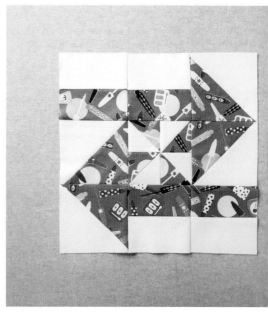

4 Cut on either side of the center seam horizontally and vertically.

5 Lay out the pieces as shown to make the rows for the block.

6 Sew the rows together to complete each block.

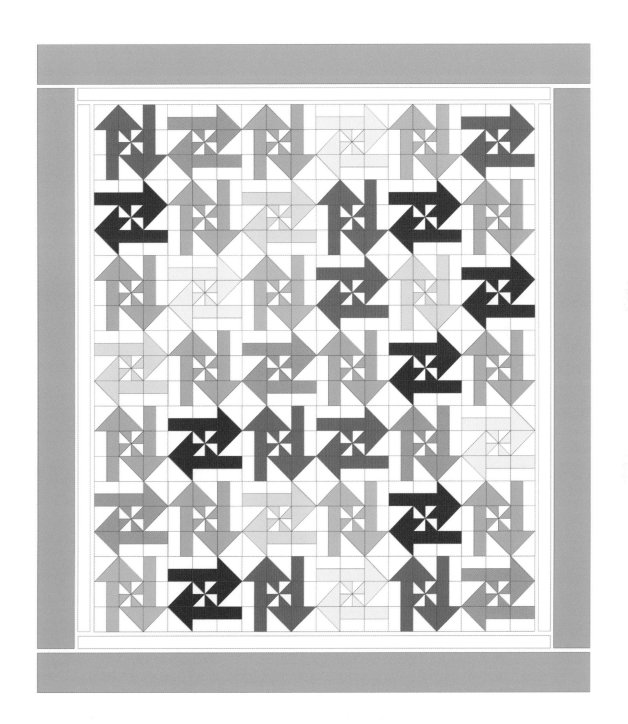

double the fun

When the snow starts to fall for the first time each winter, there's such excitement in the air. It's so magical to watch the landscape disappear under a sparkling blanket of white. Of course, not every day in winter is a wonderland. Some days are just plain cold and dreary, and you have to get a little creative to pass the time.

I remember one year when that first storm showed up early in the morning on a school day. We woke up to a nice, fluffy layer of snow, just begging to be played in. Unfortunately, time stands still for no snowman, so off to school the kids went, and that snow remained untouched.

All morning, the school was filled with antsy children, anxious to get out and play. Little did they know, the sun had already come out and was hard at work melting that precious snow. When at long last the children were let loose for recess, they poured out, hats and mittens in place, to discover only a few scattered patches of snow—certainly not enough for a decent snowman.

When the kids got home, disappointment followed them like a dark cloud. What should have been an afternoon of snow

For the tutorial and everything you need to make this quilt visit:
www.msqc.co/blockwinter17

forts and snowball fights was quickly turning dismal. What to do? I took a quick look around the room and realized just how many quilts we had and a thought struck me. The time was just right to break out the blanket forts!

Well, those kids brightened right up when they heard my suggestion. The couch was soon stripped of its cushions, all the blankets and quilts were quickly piled up and assessed, and my crew got to work suspending their haphazard building materials all over the room with a handful of clothespins. By the time it was finished, I just couldn't help myself. I crawled right inside along with them and we read books together in our cozy living room igloo.

Over the years we've experienced countless wintry days that were too cold, too windy, or too stormy for outside play. At our house, those days have become blanket fort days. After all, everything is more fun in a blanket fort! Picnics, stories, coloring books, and movie nights all become magical underneath a canopy of quilts.

A blanket fort has the power to transport you to far off lands with endless adventure, even when you are trapped inside for the day. There's always plenty of excitement to be had when you let your imagination take charge!

materials

makes an 89¾" x 102⅞" quilt

QUILT TOP
1 package 10" print squares
2 yards light background fabric
2 yards dark background fabric

BORDER
1¾ yards

BINDING
1 yard

BACKING
8¼ yards - horizontal seam(s)

SAMPLE QUILT
Soleil by Whistler Studios
for Windham Fabrics

1 cut

From the light background fabric, cut:

- (27) 2½" strips across the width of
  the fabric. Subcut each of 21 strips
  into the following rectangles – (2)
  2½" x 14" rectangles and (1) 2½"
  x 10" rectangle. Cut each of the
  remaining 6 strips into (4) 2½" x 10"
  rectangles. You will have a total of
  (42) 2½" x 14" rectangles and a total
  of (42) 2½" x 10" rectangles.

From the dark background fabric, cut:

- (27) 2½" strips across the width of
  the fabric. Subcut each of 21 strips
  into the following rectangles – (2)
  2½" x 14" rectangles and (1) 2½"
  x 10" rectangle. Cut each of the
  remaining 6 strips into (4) 2½" x 10"
  rectangles. You will have a total of
  (42) 2½" x 14" rectangles and a total
  of (42) 2½" x 10" rectangles.

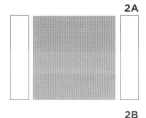
2A

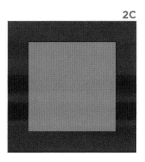
2B

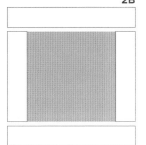
2C

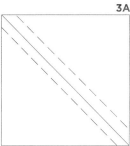
3A

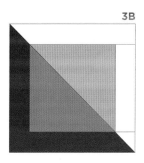
3B

2 lay out and sew

Sew a light 2½" x 10" rectangle to either side of a print 10" square. **2A**

Sew a light 2½" x 14" rectangle to the top and bottom of the square. **2B**

Make 21 blocks using the light rectangles.

Repeat the above instructions using the dark 10" rectangles on the sides and a dark 14" rectangle on the top and bottom. **Make 21 blocks.** **2C**

3 layer and sew

On each light bordered square, draw a line from corner to corner once on the diagonal. Place the marked light bordered square atop a dark bordered square with right sides facing. Sew ¼" on both sides of the drawn line. **3A**

Cut on the drawn line. Open each side to reveal a completed block. **Make 42.** **3B**

Block Size: 13⅛" Finished

4 lay out the blocks

Arrange the blocks into **7 rows** with each row made up of **6 blocks.** When you are happy with the arrangement,

sew the blocks into rows. Press the odd numbered rows toward the right and the even numbered rows toward the left. This will make the seams nest and the corners will match up more easily.

Sew the rows together.

5 borders

Cut (10) 6" strips across the width of the fabric. Sew the strips together end-to-end to make one long strip. Trim the borders from this strip.

Refer to Borders (pg. 103) in the Construction Basics to measure and cut the outer borders. The strips are approximately 92⅜" for the sides and approximately 90¼" for the top and bottom.

6 quilt and bind

Layer the quilt with batting and backing and quilt. After the quilting is complete, square up the quilt and trim away all excess batting and backing. Add binding to complete the quilt. See Construction Basics (pg. 104) for binding instructions.

1 Sew a 2½" x 10" rectangle to either side of a 10" square. Add a 2½" x 14" rectangle to the top and the bottom.

2 Half of the blocks will be bordered with dark rectangles, the remaining blocks will be bordered with light rectangles.

3 Draw a line from corner to corner once on the diagonal on the reverse side of half of the blocks. Layer a light bordered block with a dark bordered block with right sides facing. Sew on both sides of the drawn line.

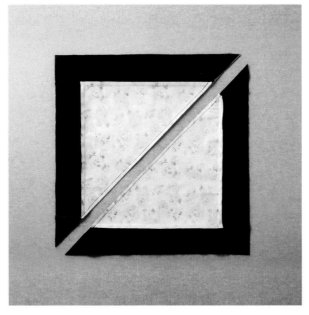

4 Cut on the drawn line.

5 Open each piece to reveal a completed block.

long
shoofly

Our family loves to build snowmen. The trouble is, we don't get very much snow in Missouri. Oh, it does snow, but usually it's only enough to cover the ground in a thin blanket of white. It gets plenty cold, we even get ice storms, but snow doesn't always show up in abundance. Of course when it does snow, it sure is pretty, almost too pretty to touch.

I love the look of a pristine, snow-covered yard. My scraggly, brown winter garden looks so much more elegant under a layer of white. However, when you have seven energetic kids at home, you can't tell them, "Kids, I know it snowed last night, but don't bother putting on your boots and mittens. I want this snow to stay untouched and perfect!" Unspotted snow is beautiful, but winter fun wins out every time.

So on snowy days in Missouri, our family heads out to make our snowmen. More often than not, we use every stitch of snow in the yard—and even then, our snowmen come out bespeckled with grass and gravel. When all's said and done, we usually end up with a shabby little family of snowmen, and a bare-naked yard. It may not be picture-perfect, but it sure is fun!

For the tutorial and everything you need to make this quilt visit:
www.msqc.co/blockwinter17

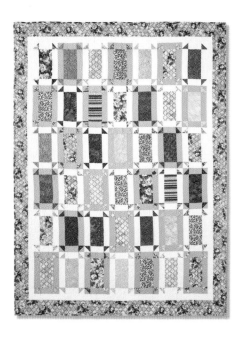

Winter can be cold and dreary, but I encourage you to try to enjoy the weather any way you can. Grab your scarf and mittens, and make the most of this magical season, especially if you're lucky enough to get a little snow!

Another favorite winter activity of ours is making snow ice cream. We carefully scoop up the fresh, clean snow and take it inside to make a batch. Add just a few simple ingredients, and you have a tasty treat, courtesy of Mother Nature!

Snow Ice Cream

1 cup milk (any kind)
1/3 cup granulated sugar
1 tsp. vanilla extract
1 pinch salt
8 cups clean snow or shaved ice (more or less depending on the density of the snow)
Optional (but strongly suggested) topping:
Sprinkles!

Mix the sugar and snow together gently and then add the milk until you have the right consistency. Finally, add the vanilla and salt to taste and as many sprinkles and you'd like. Serve immediately.

materials

makes a 72½" X 94" quilt

QUILT TOP
1 package 10" squares
2¼ yards light solid background fabric - includes inner border
1¾ yards medium solid background fabric

OUTER BORDER
1¼ yards

BINDING
¾ yard

BACKING
5¾ yards - vertical seam(s) using 42" width of fabric

SAMPLE QUILT
Peony Passion by Linnea Washburn for Northcott Fabrics

1 cut

From the package of 10" squares, cut:

- (42) squares in half for a **total of (84)** 5" x 10" rectangles. Subcut (42) 5" x 10" rectangles in half for a **total of (84)** 5" squares. Set 42 squares aside for another project.

From (42) 5" print squares, cut:

- (168) 2½" squares – you will have 4 print squares that match (1) 5" x 10" rectangle. Keep the matching prints together.

From the light solid background fabric, cut:

- (23) 2½" strips across the width of the fabric. Subcut 6 strips into 2½" x 5" rectangles for a **total of 42,** 11 strips into 2½" x 10" rectangles for a **total of 42,** and 6 strips into 2½" squares for a **total of 84.**

From the medium solid background fabric, cut:

- (23) 2½" strips across the width of the fabric. Subcut 6 strips into 2½" x 5" rectangles for a **total of 42,** 11 strips into 2½" x 10" rectangles for a **total of 42**, and 6 strips into 2½" squares for a **total of 84.**

44

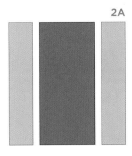

2A

2 lay out and sew

Sew a light solid background 2½" x 10" strip to either side of a print 5" x 10" rectangle. 2A

Sew matching 2½" print squares to either end of a light solid 2½" x 5" rectangle. Make 2 and sew one to the top and one to the bottom of each block. **Make 21.** 2B

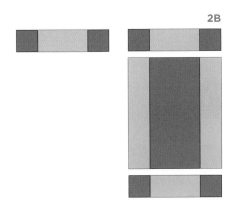

2B

Mark the sewing line on the reverse side of (84) 2½" light solid background squares. Either draw a line from corner to corner once on the diagonal or fold each square once on the diagonal and press a crease in place. Either method works for marking the line. 2C

2C

Place a 2½" marked square on one corner of the block with right sides facing. Sew on the marked line, then trim ¼" away from the sewn seam. Open and press. Repeat for the remaining 3 corners to complete 1 block.
Make 21 blocks. 2D

Repeat the above directions to make 21 blocks but use the solid medium background fabric. **Make 21 blocks.**

Block Size: 8½" x 13½" Finished

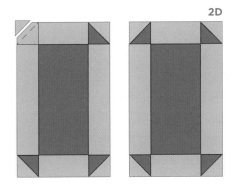

2D

3 arrange and sew

Arrange the blocks into **6 rows** with each row having **7 blocks.** Begin and end the odd numbered rows with blocks made using the light solid background pieces. Alternate the blocks edged with light background fabric with those using medium background fabric. Begin and end the even numbered rows with blocks made using the medium solid background pieces. Alternate the blocks as before. Refer to the diagram on pg. 47 if necessary.

Once you are happy with the arrangement, sew the blocks together. Press the even numbered rows toward the right and the odd numbered rows toward the left so the seams will nest.

Sew the rows together.

4 inner border

Cut (8) 2½" strips across the width of the remaining light solid background fabric. Sew the strips together end-to-end to make one long strip. Trim the borders from this strip.

Refer to Borders (pg. 103) in the Construction Basics to measure and cut the inner borders. The strips are approximately 81½" for the sides and approximately 64" for the top and bottom.

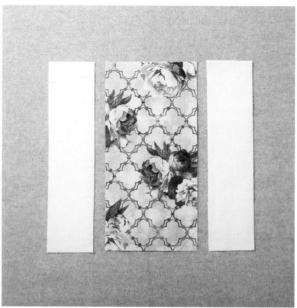

1 Sew a light 2½" x 10" rectangle to either side of a 5" x 10" print rectangle.

2 Sew a 2½" square to either end of a 2½" x 5" light rectangle. Make 2 and sew one to the top of the block and one to the bottom.

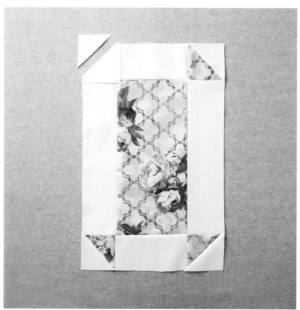

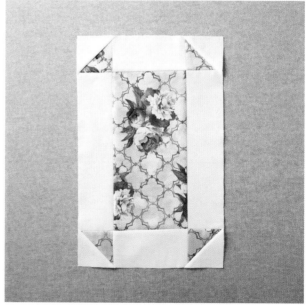

3 Place a marked 2½" square on each corner of the block. Sew on the marked line, then trim the excess fabric away ¼" from the sewn seam.

4 Make half of the blocks using light solid rectangles surrounding the center print rectangles. Make the other half using medium solid rectangles.

5 outer border

Cut (8) 5″ strips across the width of the fabric. Sew the strips together end-to-end to make one long strip. Trim the borders from this strip.

Refer to Borders (pg. 103) in the Construction Basics to measure and cut the outer borders. The strips are approximately 85½″ for the sides and approximately 73″ for the top and bottom.

6 quilt and bind

Layer the quilt with batting and backing and quilt. After the quilting is complete, square up the quilt and trim away all excess batting and backing. Add binding to complete the quilt. See the Construction Basics (pg. 104) for binding instructions.

mini
tumbler

Baking bread isn't something many people do anymore. It's a process that takes a bit of time and effort, but the result is absolutely worth it. For me, it parallels my love of quilting. Homemade is always my favorite and whether I'm making quilts or baking bread, it gives me great satisfaction to make something from scratch.

When I was young, my grandmother would have a "baking day" once a week and I was always eager to help her. Every Tuesday we would mix up dough for an assortment of delicious home-baked goods and the house would be filled with the aroma of rolls, breads, and cookies. As she kneaded the dough, I watched her strong arms working and wondered if I'd ever be big enough to make bread just like her.

Then, when I had a family of my own, I returned to my roots and began making bread again in earnest. With many little hungry mouths to feed, baking our own bread was economical and provided a great outlet for my creativity. And the kids loved it. As I homeschooled them, they learned right

For the tutorial and everything you need to make this quilt visit:
www.msqc.co/blockwinter17

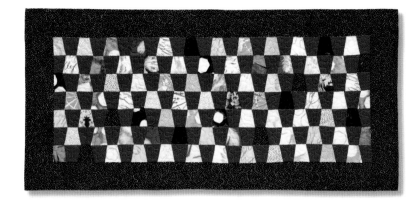

alongside me and would help me shape rolls and knead dough. They were always so capable and quick to help. Sure, the floor might be covered in flour by the time we were through, but it was worth the mess!

Of course things didn't always go as planned. Once, when I was in a rush, I completely forgot to add the yeast. I never proof the yeast first—I know, it's shocking! I add in the wet ingredients, and a little flour, and then put the yeast right into the mixture. It proofs just fine in the dough itself and saves me a bit of time. Well, this time around, I just plain forgot. The dough felt right in my hands and was shiny when I was done kneading it, but when I checked it after an hour, it hadn't risen at all. So, that week we improvised and had flatbread sandwiches instead!

The great thing about being creative is that life becomes much more interesting instead of frustrating. Instead of viewing flatbread as a failure, I embraced it instead and it turned out great. I like to remember the same thing when I'm quilting. As the saying goes, "there are no mistakes, only variations!" In turn, many new ideas are born and patterns become the jumping off point for new adventures.

Being creative is an important part of life and making food for the people I love and quilts to keep them warm just feels right. Perfection doesn't communicate that love more fully, so I allow my mistakes to remain. The next time your bread goes flat, or your corners don't match up just right, or whatever it may be, just remember, you've now made a new, interesting variation!

Mama Hawk's
CINNAMON ROLL
—— RECIPE ——

Dough:
2 Tbsp. yeast
½ cup warm water (110°)
1 Tbsp. granulated sugar
1 cup warm milk (110°)
⅓ cup unsalted butter
⅓ cup granulated sugar
2 tsp. salt
2 large eggs, well beaten
4-5 cups unsifted flour

Filling:
1 cup salted butter, softened
1½ cups brown sugar
1 Tbsp. flour
2½ Tbsp. ground cinnamon

Cream Cheese Icing:
1 cup salted butter, softened
8 oz package of cream cheese
2 tsp. vanilla
4-5 cups powdered sugar

Sprinkle yeast and 1 tablespoon of sugar into the warm water. Set aside until yeast becomes foamy. In a small saucepan, melt the butter. Add the milk, sugar, and salt. Keep it over low heat until warmed to around 110°. Using a large mixer with a dough hook attachment, add 3 cups of flour. Mix in the yeast mixture. Then add the milk mixture, mixing until combined. Add the eggs. Gradually add the remaining flour (up to 5 cups) until the dough comes together but remains slightly sticky. Pour dough into a large greased bowl. Cover with plastic wrap and refrigerate overnight. Two and a half hours before serving time, remove dough from the refrigerator. Turn out onto a floured surface, and knead until it's nice and smooth. Form into a rectangle, and then roll out into a larger rectangle keeping a ¼" thickness. Make filling by combining all ingredients and mixing until smooth and spreadable. Spread filling onto the rolled out dough. Cover the entire surface. Roll up the dough lengthwise from the long side of the rectangle. Pinch the seam into the dough at the end. Using a sharp serrated knife, cut the rolled dough log in half, then slice each side in half again so you have 4 separate logs. Slice each log into 3rds, making 12 rolls. Place each sliced roll into a 9 x 13 pan coated with cooking spray, four rows with three across. Lightly cover with a dishtowel and let rise in a warm place until doubled in size (approx. 2 hours). Make the cream cheese icing, set aside. Bake at 400° for 9-10 mins. Slather with cream cheese icing, then get lost in warm fluffy cinnamon roll heaven!

VARIATIONS

Dinner Rolls: Make the same dough, but instead of the brown sugar filling, slather the rolled out dough with softened salted butter. Roll them up, slice, and place each slice in a buttered muffin tin. Let them rise and then bake. Serve them with fresh homemade raspberry jam.

Orange Rolls: Do the same as the above variation, but sprinkle sugar onto the butter and add fresh orange zest.

materials

makes a 20" X 40½" table runner

TABLE RUNNER TOP
2 packages – 42 ct. 2½" print
   squares *or* 1 package 5" print
   squares
½ yard background fabric

BORDER
½ yard

BINDING
¼ yard

BACKING
1½ yards

ADDITIONAL SUPPLIES
MSQC Mini Tumbler Template

SAMPLE QUILT
Black and White by Jennifer
Sampou for Robert Kaufman

1 cut

If you are using 5" squares, cut each square in half vertically making 2½" x 5" rectangles. Set one set of rectangles aside. Use the Mini Tumbler Template to cut 2 shapes from each rectangle for a total of 84. If you are using the 2½" squares, cut 1 tumbler shape from each square for a **total of 84**.

From the background fabric, cut:

- (5) 2½" strips across the width of the fabric. Subcut each strip into 20 tumblers for a **total of 84.** With each cut, flip the template 180 degrees to get more pieces per strip.

2A

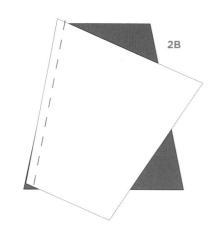

2B

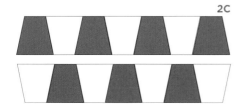

2C

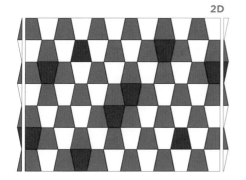

2D

2 lay out and sew

Lay out the tumblers in rows. Each row has **12 background tumblers and 12 print tumblers.** The background tumblers alternate with the prints. **2A**

Using a ¼" seam allowance, sew the tumblers together side-to-side into rows, alternating a print tumbler with a background tumbler. Offset the tumblers by ¼" as shown to create "dog ears" to ensure the tumblers are aligned in a straight row. Flip every other tumbler 180 degrees. **2B**

Make 7 rows. Make **4 rows** that begin with a print tumbler and **3 rows** that begin with a background tumbler. Press the seam allowances of the odd numbered rows toward the right and the even numbered rows toward the left. Sew the rows together. **2C**

Trim the zigzag ends off evenly, using a rotary cutter and ruler. **2D**

3 border

Cut (3) 3½" strips across the width of the fabric. Sew the strips together end-to-end to make one long strip. Trim the borders from this strip.

Refer to Borders (pg. 103) in the Construction Basics to measure and cut the outer borders. The strips are approximately 14½" for the ends and approximately 41" for the top and bottom.

4 quilt and bind

Layer the quilt with batting and backing and quilt. After the quilting is complete, square up the quilt and trim away all excess batting and backing. Add binding to complete the quilt. See Construction Basics (pg. 104) for binding instructions.

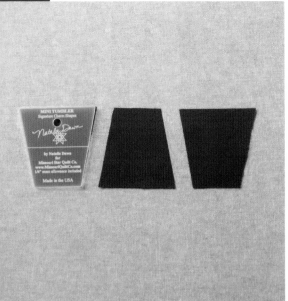

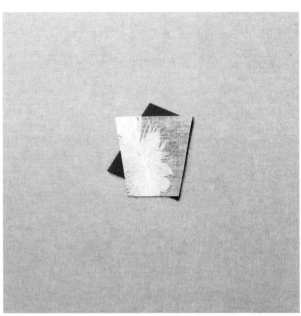

1 Use the MSQC Mini Tumbler Template to cut the pieces for the table runner. Flip the template end to end while cutting

2 Offset the pieces by ¼" to ensure the tumblers are aligned in a straight row.

3 Alternate a background tumbler with a print tumbler when sewing the pieces together.

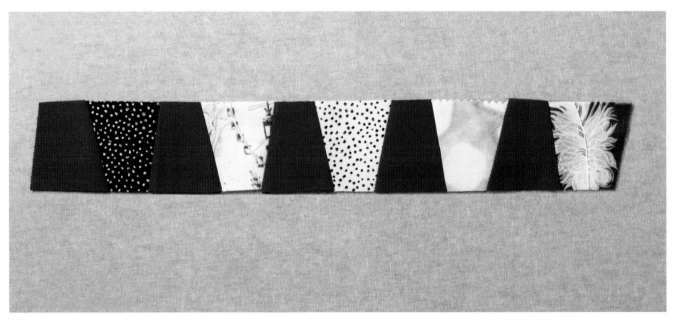

4 Press the seam allowances of the even numbered rows in the opposite direction of the odd numbered rows to make your seams nest.

For the tutorial and everything you need to make this quilt visit:
www.msqc.co/blockwinter17

periwinkle

Girls' night is all about getting together with your best friends, cutting loose, and remembering all the things you love about each other. It's almost like a trip back in time—you can forget about the responsibilities in your life and spend a moment suspended in girlish excitement. For me, a good girls' night doesn't happen very often, but when it does, hold onto your hats, ladies!

When my kids were little, my mother, my sister, and I decided to take a girls trip to Utah. This girls' night was going on the road! All the way there we sang our favorite show tunes, stopped for plenty of snacks, and let our hair fly around with no regard for open windows. It was a sweet break from the everyday and we were going to make the most of it.

Now my idea of a party is pretty tame. I like to relax at home in my sewing room, or perhaps cuddled up with a good book. You're probably going to get a chuckle out of this, but we were headed to Utah to do a bit of family history research, my favorite thing besides quilting. I love exploring my roots and finding out where I came from. Family is everything to me, and I enjoy getting to know my ancestors.

So the plan was to take a trip out to the big Family History Library in downtown Salt Lake City. That place is just incredible! It holds millions of records and anyone can go there

and do research for free. I was in heaven. We spent a good portion of our time there, happily sifting through microfilm and making small discoveries.

When we were through, the next stop was to go visit one of our dear old friends, Alice. We surprised her at her work and she was elated! We all decided to continue our visit at Alice's home so she told us to follow her in her car. Now, this was in the days before GPS and cell phones, so you can imagine what might happen next.

As we followed Alice's car in the dark, tail lights blurred together and we hadn't realized that we'd lost her. So, we kept following what we thought was Alice's car. We followed this car for what seemed like forever, laughing and joking all the way, when suddenly the car stopped. A man got out of the car and turned to look at us in a strange way. He had no idea why a group of giggling women had been following him all this time! He tentatively asked, "Why were you following me?" Well, that really set us off! We laughed and laughed as his suspicion turned into a smile. When we finally calmed down enough to tell him what had happened, he kindly let us use his phone to find out where Alice actually lived and soon we were on our way again.

Boy, things were different in the days before cell phones! You could really get yourself into a pickle back then. Eventually, we made it just fine to Alice's home, after our little detour, and she just shook her head in disbelief. I guess you had to be there! It's still one of my favorite road trip memories. The key is, no matter what goes wrong, if you keep laughing, things'll turn out just fine.

materials

makes a 58" x 70" quilt

QUILT TOP
2 packages 5" print squares
3¾ yards background fabric

BORDER
1 yard

BINDING
¾ yard

BACKING
3¾ yards - horizontal seam(s)

ADDITIONAL SUPPLIES
1 package MSQC Wacky Web
    Triangle Papers
1 MSQC Small Periwinkle Template
    for 5" squares
Glue Stick - optional

SAMPLE QUILT
On Trend by Jen Allyson for
Riley Blake

1 cut

Select (80) 5" squares from the 2 packs. Using the Periwinkle Template, cut 1 shape from each. (There will be 4 squares left over for another project.)

From the background fabric, cut:

- (20) 6½" strips across the width of the fabric. Subcut the strips into 5" x 6½" rectangles for a **total of 160.**

2 block construction

Each block is made up of 4 triangular units. If you are using the glue stick, add a dab of glue to the reverse side of a print periwinkle shape. Place the shape on top of a paper triangle in the corner with the right side of the fabric facing up. If you are not using a glue stick, pin the shape to the paper triangle. **2A**

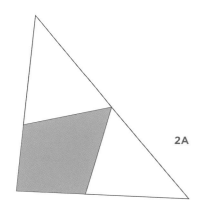

2A

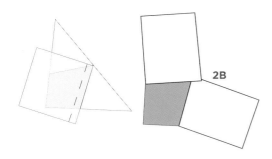

2B

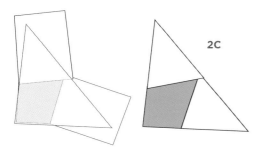

2C

2D

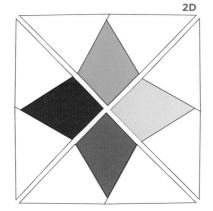

Align the edge of a background rectangle with the edge of the periwinkle shape with right sides facing. Sew in place, using a ¼" seam allowance. Repeat for the other side of the triangle. **2B**

Press the triangle unit. Turn over and trim the excess fabric evenly with the triangle paper. **Make 4** per block. **2C**

Lay out 4 triangle units. Remove the paper and sew the units together to complete 1 block. **Make 20. 2D**

Block Size: 12" Finished

3 lay out and sew

Lay out the blocks in rows with each row having **4 blocks. Make 5 rows.** Press the seam allowances of the even numbered rows toward the left and the odd numbered rows toward the right. This will make the seams nest and the corners match more easily.

Sew the rows together to complete the center of the quilt.

4 border

Cut (6) 5½" strips across the width of the fabric. Sew the strips together end-to-end to make one long strip. Trim the borders from this strip.

Refer to Borders (pg. 103) in the Construction Basics to measure and cut the outer borders. The strips are approximately 60½" for the sides and approximately 58½" for the top and bottom.

5 quilt and bind

Layer the quilt with batting and backing and quilt. After the quilting is complete, square up the quilt and trim away all excess batting and backing. Add binding to complete the quilt. See Construction Basics (pg. 104) for binding instructions.

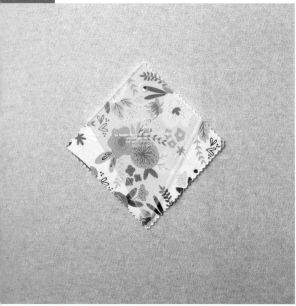

1 Use the MSQC Small Periwinkle Template to cut shapes from 5″ squares.

2 Place the periwinkle shape on top of a paper triangle in the corner with the right side of the fabric facing up.

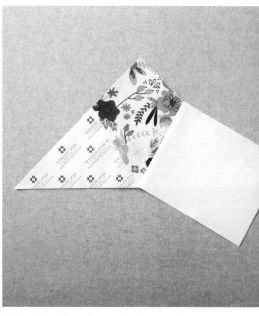

3 Align the edge of a background rectangle with the edge of the periwinkle shape with right sides facing. Sew in place, using a ¼″ seam allowance.

4 Add another rectangle to the other side of the periwinkle shape and sew in place as before. Press.

5 Trim each section evenly with the paper.

6 Sew 4 periwinkle sections together to complete the block.

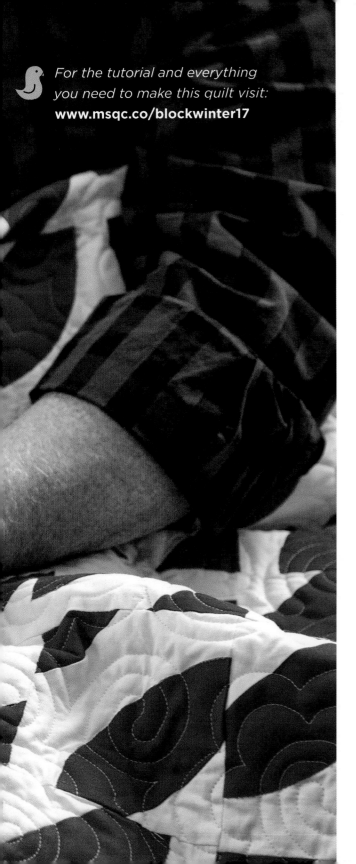

For the tutorial and everything you need to make this quilt visit:
www.msqc.co/blockwinter17

cornered
drunkard's path

I grew up with parents who always held hands, so Ron and I hold hands too. Whether we are strolling through town or watching a movie, and even when we're driving, I like to reach over and rest my hand on his. Anytime we are close enough, you'll probably see us holding hands. It's such a simple thing to do, but it means so much.

I have had people say to me, "I love that you hold hands. It's so sweet!" After many years, however, it has become as much habit as it is a display of affection, just like small children reach up instinctively for their parent's hand when it's time to cross a road. It's nice to know that I have a constant companion, and it just seems natural to reach out for one another.

When we were first married, Ron was a mechanic, and later on he worked as a machinist. During those years, his hands were always cut and bruised, and no matter how hard he scrubbed, he could never get the grease out from under his fingernails completely. Sometimes, in those early years, I would look at his hands and wonder how I could ever get him properly cleaned up. It seemed like a chore to make him presentable for church or a night on the town, but looking back, it really didn't matter all that much.

As I grew older, and a little wiser, those work-worn hands became beautiful to me. After seeing the struggles Ron went through to provide for our family, they came to represent the sacrifices he made for all of us. That meant so much more than a well-manicured hand to me.

Now that Ron does more machine quilting than mechanic work, his hands are softer and unstained, but they still hold the same love and kindness. He has held my hand every step of the way as we embarked on this

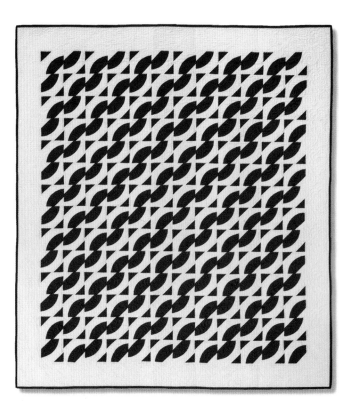

grand journey together, and his help and support is so precious to me. Whenever I need a little encouragement, he gives my hand a squeeze and urges me forward.

The other day I happened to notice how old our hands look together. I was surprised to realize how like my mother's hand mine had become. When did that happen? As the years have come and gone, our hands mark the passage of time and yet they still work together as well as ever. Although my hand might have a few wrinkles and age spots, I am so thankful that he holds it still.

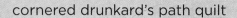

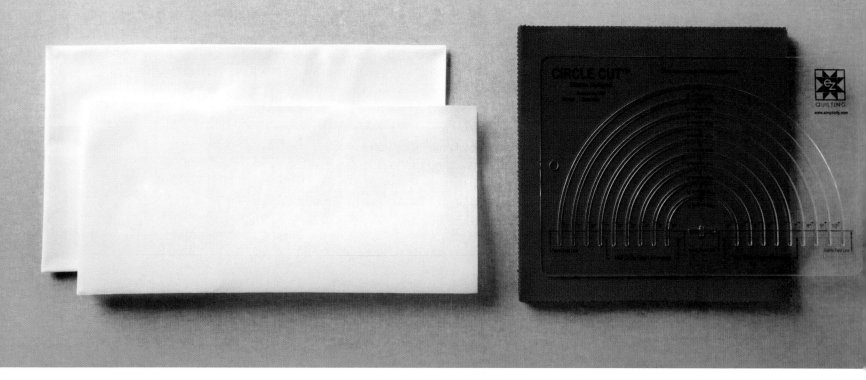

materials

makes a 64" X 73" quilt

QUILT TOP
2¾ yards solid
5 yards background – includes outer
  border

BINDING
¾ yard

BACKING
4 yards (42" wide) – horizontal
  seam(s)

ADDITIONAL SUPPLIES
3 yards 24" wide Fusible Interfacing
  (We used Steam-a-Seam 2 Lite)
Easy Circle Cut Ruler

SAMPLE QUILT
Cotton Supreme Solids - Redwork
and Optical White by RJR Fabrics

1 cut

From the solid fabric, cut:

- (9) 7½" strips across the width of
  the fabric – subcut each of the strips
  into (5) 7½" squares for a **total of
  42 squares.**

- (11) 2½" strips across the width of
  the fabric - subcut each of the strips
  into (16) 2½" squares. You need a
  total of 168 squares.

From the background fabric, cut:

- (11) 10" strips across the width of the
  fabric – subcut each strip into (4)
  10" squares. You need a **total of 42.**

- (11) 2½" strips across the width of
  the fabric - subcut each of the strips
  into (16) 2½" squares. You need a
  total of 168 squares.

Set aside the remaining background
fabric for the outer border.

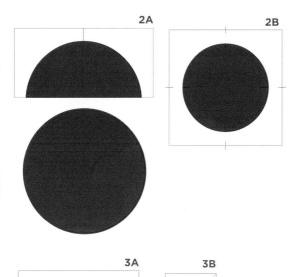

2A

2B

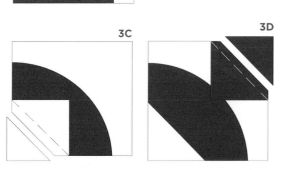

3A

3B

3C

3D

3E

2 fuse, mark and cut

Press the solid background squares to the fusible interfacing and trim the fusible evenly with the edges of each square. Turn each square over so the paper side is up. Place the Easy Circle Cut Ruler on the paper backing and draw a half circle using the 7" slot. Fold the square in half and cut on the drawn line. When you unfold the piece, you will have a 7" circle. **2A**

Tear off the paper backing from the circle. Center the circle on the 10" background square and press in place.

 NOTE: *If you fold your background square in half horizontally and vertically and finger press the crease in place, you will be able to center the circle easily by aligning the fold of the circle with the fold of the square.* **2B**

Cut circles in the same manner from the remaining red squares and fuse each to a 10" background square.

When all circles have been fused in place, stitch around each circle using a small zig zag or a blanket stitch.

3 cut and sew

Cut each 10" square in half vertically and horizontally. You will end up with (4) 5" squares. **3A**

Pick up 4 background 2½" squares and 4 solid 2½" squares. Fold each square from corner to corner once on the diagonal. Finger press the crease in place. The crease will mark your sewing line. **3B**

Place a background square on the corner of the red portion of a 5" square with right sides facing. Sew on the creased line. Trim the excess fabric away ¼" from the sewn seam. **3C**

Place a red 2½" square on the corner of the background portion of the 5" square with right sides facing. Sew on the creased line. Trim the excess fabric away ¼" from the sewn seam. **3D**

Repeat for the remaining (3) 5" squares.

Sew the 4 squares together as shown to complete one block. Make a **total of 42 blocks.** **3E**

Block Size: 9" Finished

4 arrange and sew

Arrange the blocks into rows with each row made up of **6 blocks.** Make **7 rows.** Press the odd numbered rows toward

1 Fuse a red circle to the background square. Stitch in place using a small blanket stitch.

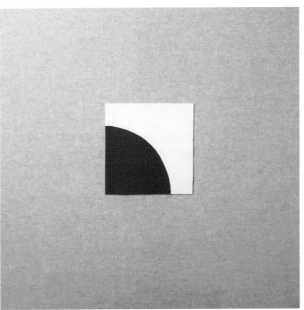

2 Cut each 10″ square in half vertically and horizontally.

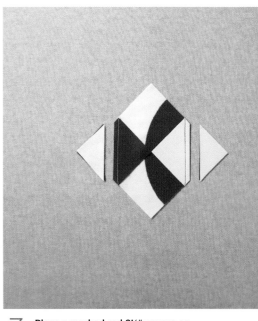

3 Place a marked red 2½″ square on the white corner of the block and a marked white 2½″ square on the red corner. Sew on the marked line, then trim the excess fabric away ¼″ from the sewn seam.

4 Lay out 4 squares in a 4-patch grid.

5 Sew the 4 squares together to complete the block.

the right and the even numbered rows toward the left to make your seams nest easily.

Sew the rows together.

5 border

Cut (7) 5½" strips across the width of the fabric. Sew the strips together end-to-end to make one long strip. Trim the borders from this strip.

Refer to Borders (pg. 103) in the Construction Basics to measure and cut the outer borders. The strips are approximately 63½" for the sides and approximately 64½" for the top and bottom.

6 quilt and bind

Layer the quilt with batting and backing and quilt. After the quilting is complete, square up the quilt and trim away all excess batting and backing. Add binding to complete the quilt. See Construction Basics (pg. 104) for binding instructions.

simple diamonds

I love live music. There's something about it that fills me with excitement and energy. Whether I'm walking in the city and hear a street musician thumping out a rhythm on plastic drums or strolling in the park and someone's playing the guitar with a group of friends, I have the urge to start dancing and singing along with them! Ron's always a good sport and every now and then he indulges my love of music with a night out together at a concert.

Recently, we had the chance to go see one of our favorite singers on his farewell tour. It was such a thrilling night. There are very few musicians that span generations and this artist is one of the greats. I remember my dad singing his songs when I was a child and, as I grew up, he continued making music that became meaningful to Ron and I throughout our marriage.

When this aged superstar came on stage, he seemed to be in pain as he walked very slowly to the center and sat on a stool. The lights were dimmed and the spotlight was on him. Then, as he started singing, after only a few lines, he lowered his microphone because he seemed to have forgotten the words. We were stunned, but he persevered and kept trying to sing. Pretty soon, we all started singing along and if he happened

For the tutorial and everything you need to make this quilt visit:
www.msqc.co/blockwinter17

to forget a word or two, the audience would sing it for him! Then he'd pick up his microphone again and keep on going with a smile on his face. This went on for the whole concert. It was almost like listening to a record skip. He sounded amazing and we didn't mind a little static.

At one point he paused to look out at us and said, "It's the weirdest thing, one day you wake up and you are old!" He explained his limping gait saying that he'd had a knee replaced recently and he swore it was the wrong knee! His humor kept us chuckling all night long and our hearts swelled with even greater love for him and his music. There are always a few concertgoers who can yell over the roar of the crowd and speak for all of us saying, "We love you!" It's amazing how after hearing an iconic song, it becomes even more meaningful to you than before, hearing it there in person, rather than the perfect radio-friendly version on an album.

After hearing a song that I'd sung to Ron almost our whole married life, we were filled with emotion. It's incredible how much music affects us as it's woven in and through our lives. I love the art that is within all of us. We are all capable of creating beauty, no matter who we are. Whether we are painters, singers, or quilters, we are all artists in our own right and what we create can be life-changing.

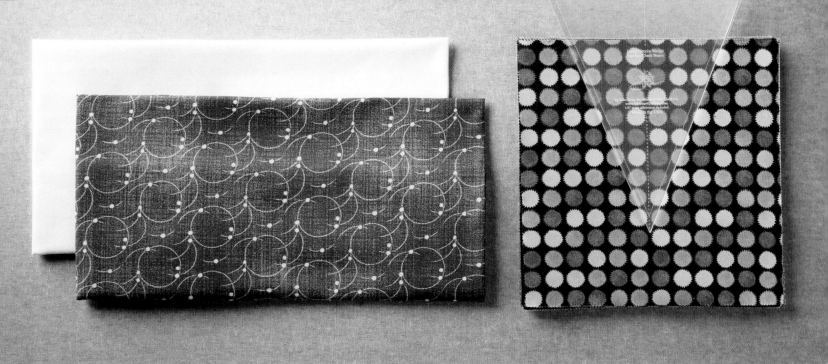

materials

makes a 60" X 73¾" quilt

QUILT TOP
package 10" squares
1¼ yards background – includes
   inner border

OUTER BORDER
1¼ yards

BINDING
¾ yard

BACKING
4½ yards - vertical seam(s)

ADDITIONAL SUPPLIES
MSQC Large Simple Wedge Template

SAMPLE QUILT
Aubade: a Song to the Dawn by
Janet Clare for Moda

1 cut

From each 10" square, cut:

- 2 triangles using the Large Simple
  Wedge Template.
  (See diagram **1A** for template
  placement.) Keep the matching
  triangles stacked together. You will
  have a **total of 84 triangles.** **1A**

From the background fabric, cut:

- (2) 9¼" strips across the width of
  the fabric – subcut the strips into
  triangles using the Large Simple
  Wedge Template. Flip the template
  end to end as you cut to make the
  best use of your fabric. You need a
  total of 14 triangles. Set the
  remaining fabric aside for the
  inner border. **1B**

1A

1B

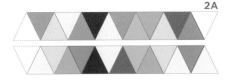

2A

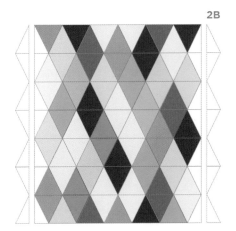

2B

2 lay out and sew

Lay out the triangles before sewing. In order to create the diamonds, you will need to place the matching triangles one above the other as you make your rows.

Sew the triangles into rows. Each row will begin and end with a background triangle. **Make 7 rows** being aware of the color placement of each triangle. **2A**

Sew the rows together.

After the rows are sewn together, trim the excess background triangles on each side of the quilt, leaving ¼" seam allowance. **2B**

3 inner border

Cut (6) 3" strips across the width of the fabric. Sew the strips together end-to-end to make one long strip. Trim the borders from this strip.

Refer to Borders (pg. 103) in the Construction Basics to measure and cut the inner borders. The strips are approximately 58¼" for the sides and approximately 49½" for the top and bottom.

4 outer border

Cut (7) 6" strips across the width of the fabric. Sew the strips together end-to-end to make one long strip. Trim the borders from this strip.

Refer to Borders (pg. 103) in the Construction Basics to measure and cut the outer borders. The strips are approximately 63¼" for the sides and approximately 60½" for the top and bottom.

5 quilt and bind

Layer the quilt with batting and backing and quilt. After the quilting is complete, square up the quilt and trim away all excess batting and backing. Add binding to complete the quilt. See Construction Basics (pg. 104) for binding instructions.

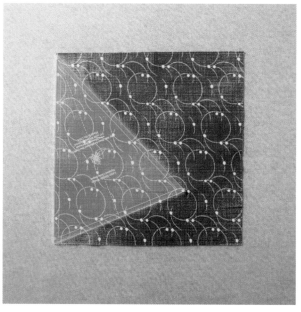

1 Place the MSQC Large Simple Wedge Template on a 10″ square, aligning the long side of the template with the edge of the square.

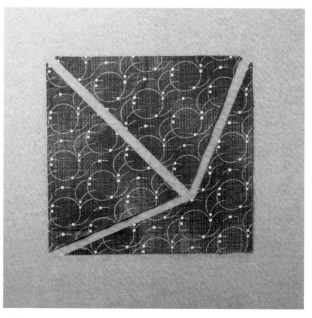

2 Cut 2 triangles from each 10″ square.

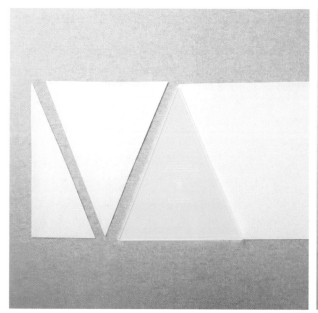

4 Subcut 9¼″ strips of background fabric using the template. Flip the template 180° as when cutting to get the most cuts from a strip.

5 Lay out the triangles in rows before sewing. Matching triangles need to be placed one above the other to create the look of diamonds.

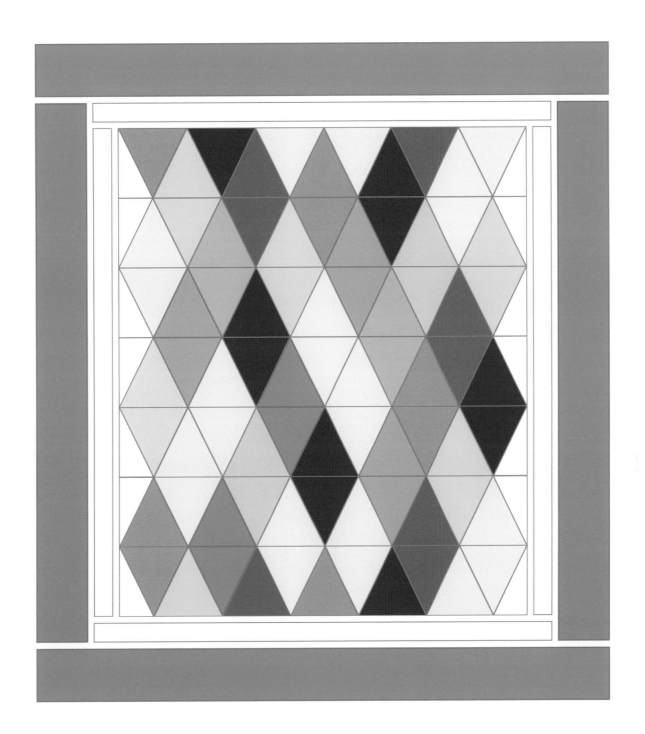

super easy
hourglass

Recently, while looking through some old family photos, I came across this amazing picture of Ron and myself on Ellis Island. Our children are sitting close by, and the towers of the World Trade Center are in the background. We had gone to see the Statue of Liberty and decided to make a stop at Ellis Island to find our ancestors' names on the American Immigrant Wall of Honor. I have always loved learning about my family history, so it was quite a thrill to see those names engraved on the memorial.

I'd heard the story of my family's arrival a hundred times, but it suddenly became very real. In 1912, my maternal grandmother and her family boarded a ship called "The Cedric" to embark on a great journey from Sweden to America. They arrived at Ellis Island where they, along with thousands of other immigrants, were ushered through long, slow-moving processing lines.

For most immigrants, the procedure was simple, and they passed through inspection with no trouble. Individuals with any sort of illness or infirmity, however, were flagged for further screening. If there were signs of contagious disease

For the tutorial and everything you need to make this quilt visit:
www.msqc.co/blockwinter17

or weakness in the mind or body, admittance might be denied. I can't even imagine the worry they must have felt as they waited anxiously to find out if they would be allowed to enter the country.

When my ancestors reached the front of the line, my aunt Linnea was found to have some kind of eye infection, and she was brought into a separate room so she could be evaluated. It was a frightening time for the family. They worried that she would not be allowed into the country, and the entire family would be forced to travel all the way back to Sweden. Fortunately, Linnea was cleared and they were allowed to enter the United States together.

When I stepped up to the wall and saw Linnea's name engraved in the stone, I felt a rush of gratitude. She really

had been here with her family, in this very spot, and by some miracle they were given permission to stay. A feeling of pride swelled in my heart, and I felt profound gratitude for the blessing of living in America.

That feeling of patriotism has never left me, and while I don't consider myself to be a particularly political person, I love this country with all my heart. There is so much good and so much potential here. It's certainly not a perfect place, but I believe in doing my part to make it a little better so that the generations that follow can look back at my footsteps and say, "Thank you for paving the way."

materials

makes a 64¾" X 64¾" quilt

QUILT TOP
4 packages 5" squares

INNER BORDER
½ yard

OUTER BORDER
1¼ yards

BINDING
½ yard

BACKING
4 yards - vertical seam(s)

SAMPLE QUILT
Handmaker by Natalie Barnes of
Beyond the Reef for Windham Fabrics

1 sew

Select 4 contrasting squares and sew

them together to make a 4-patch unit.

Make 42. 1A

Select (2) 4-patch units and

place them together with right sides

facing. Sew all around the outside edge

using a ¼" seam allowance. Repeat,

using the remaining 4-patch units. 1B

Cut each sewn pair of 4-patch units from

corner to corner twice on the diagonal.

1A

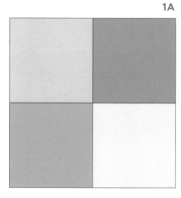

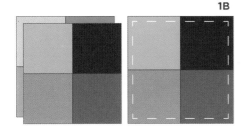

1B

Open and press. Square each block to 6¼". Repeat for the remaining units. You will have a **total of 84 hourglass blocks.** 1C

Block Size: 5¾" Finished

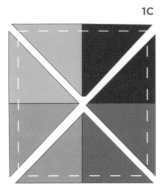

1C

2 lay out and sew

Arrange the blocks in **9 rows**. Each row is made up of **9 blocks**. When you are happy with the arrangement, sew the blocks together. Press the seam allowances of the odd numbered rows toward the left and the even numbered rows toward the right. This will make your seams nest and it will be easier to match up the corners. Sew the rows together.

We made our quilt using **81 of our blocks.** You'll have 3 hourglass blocks left for another project.

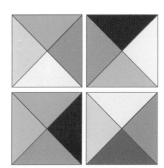

3 inner border

Cut (6) 2½" strips across the width of the fabric. Sew the strips together end-to-end to make one long strip. Trim the borders from this strip.

Refer to Borders (pg. 103) in the Construction Basics to measure and cut the inner borders. The strips are approximately 52¼" for the sides and approximately 56¼" for the top and bottom.

4 outer border

Cut (7) 5" strips across the width of the fabric. Sew the strips together end-to-end to make one long strip. Trim the borders from this strip. Refer to Borders (pg. 103) in the Construction Basics to measure and cut the outer borders. The strips are approximately 56¼" for the sides and approximately 65¼" for the top and bottom.

5 quilt and bind

Layer the quilt with batting and backing and quilt. After the quilting is complete, square up the quilt and trim away all excess batting and backing. Add binding to complete the quilt. See Construction Basics (pg. 104) for binding instructions.

1 Lay out (4) 5″ squares in a 4-patch formation.

2 Sew the 4 squares together.

3 Layer one 4-patch atop another with right sides facing.

4 Sew all the way around the outer perimeter of the layered 4-patches. Cut from corner to corner twice on the diagonal.

5 Layer one 4-patch atop another with right sides facing.

couch to quilt

I'm always trying to spread the joy of quilting wherever I go, and one day I realized that we needed to do more to make this wonderful world of quilting more accessible to everyone! That's why I'm so excited to introduce you to a new program called Couch to Quilt. It's like nothing we've ever done before. Jumping right in and making a quilt from scratch can seem really overwhelming, so we broke it down into simple steps that make it more approachable and we've included everything you need (except the sewing machine) to help you make your very own quilt, including machine quilting and binding.

I'm fond of saying, "Begin where you are." You're on a creative journey and no matter where you are in life, you can always learn something new. If you've been struggling to find success quilting or if you've always wanted to make a quilt, but aren't sure where to begin, this is a great place to start.

Couch to Quilt is also wonderful for sharing the joy of quilting with people you love. I guarantee you'll see a smile on your loved one's face when they open up this incredible box full of goodness.

So, if you've been teetering on the edge, trying to get into quilting and you need a little boost, or maybe you have a friend who'd like to give quilting a whirl, this is your answer! And don't worry, I'll be there right alongside you, guiding you from beginning to end. I think you'll be amazed at what you can do!

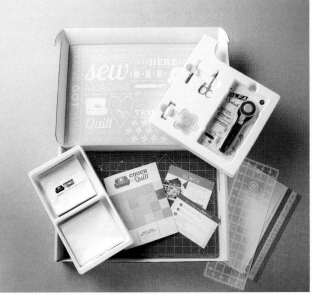

1 This cute little box will arrive at your doorstep.

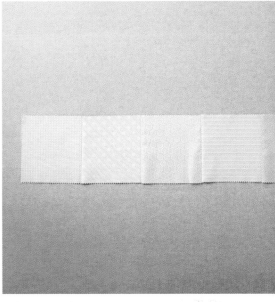

2 Open the box to see everything you need to make your first quilt. When you finish send your top back to us to be quilted and bound for free!

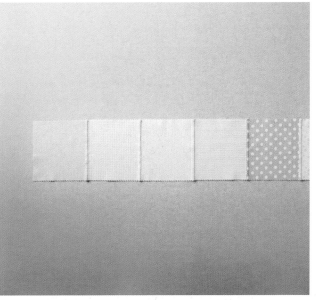

3 Sew (5) 5″ squares together to make a row.

4 Press the seams of the odd numbered rows toward the right.

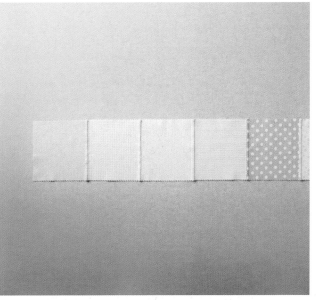

5 Press the seam allowances of the even numbered rows toward the left.

6 Sew the rows together. Notice how the seam allowances nest together. The corners line up so much more easily!

Quilt Tales
- a quilt along story -

Have you ever wondered what stories a quilt might tell? Do you find yourself daydreaming, longing for a little adventure? Let yourself be transported to a place outside of time and reality, and get lost in a magical world we've created just for you. Our favorite fairy tales have inspired us to create a unique quilting experience called "Quilt Tales." Each issue of BLOCK Magazine this year will contain a new chapter in a story to complement a quilt pattern. Stitch along with us and let your imagination run free!

The Forest Bride
By Nichole Spravzoff

BLOCK ONE
THE FEAST OF VALBORG

Ingrid knelt on the floor next to the carved cedar chest her father had made for her dowry and pulled out a beautiful quilt pieced with blue and white pinwheels. It was an understated pattern, but all of the tiny stitches, placed with such care, made it into something much more than a blanket. She traced the designs with her fingers and then held it tightly to her chest, inhaling the warm scent of the wood. She meant to put the quilt back into the box and then hesitated. *Why shouldn't I use it?* She thought to herself. *It's not like I'll ever be married.*

Ingrid's mother, Agnes, had made the quilt for her when she was betrothed to Ivar, Ingrid's childhood sweetheart. Agnes was beloved and wise. Whenever the villagers had needed a little extra luck, they turned to her. Clothes mended by her hands held together longer. Blankets stitched by her kept children warm and quiet at night. When a couple was to be wed, they turned to Agnes for a quilt that would ensure a happy and prosperous marriage. Everything she made was filled with love, and perhaps a touch of enchantment.

Sadly, Agnes never lived to see her daughter's marriage, and seven years had passed since the quilt was made, yet it still resided in the cedar chest, waiting to be used. All of Ingrid's youthful hopes seemed to sit with it, undisturbed and unfulfilled. Ivar had been the love of her life and they'd pledged to get married. But it wasn't to be. He lost his life in a hunting accident before they could be married. Now Ingrid was well past the age most girls were married and she continued on with her life. Ivar's loss had been devastating to her and the other men in the village paled in comparison, so she did the best she could. She was content with her life and soon found herself absorbed in the work her mother had passed on to her. Ingrid made beautiful things from simple cloth and thread and they filled her life with peace. Many in the village came to see her as somewhat of a widow, although they treated her kindly. There was pity lingering in their voices as they remarked on her skill and grace, lamenting that she'd never share her life with another, but her response to their concern was always a joke or a lighthearted comment. Ingrid was different than most.

Spring had arrived in Ingrid's small village and the day had finally come to celebrate the Feast of Valborg. It was one of her favorite holidays. It meant the end of the cold, dark winter and sweeter days to come. There would be picnics in the meadow and a bonfire at night. Then they would all gather together and sing songs to welcome the new season. It brought back memories from her youth. She recalled wearing a crown of flowers in her raven hair and a dress that her mother had made with a red embroidered bodice that laced up the middle and a yellow skirt the color of buttercups. She'd never wondered who would sit next to her at the picnic. It was always Ivar. They had fallen in love as they'd grown up together. Now she wore one of her mother's dresses, a midnight blue smock, cinched with a black apron that almost reached the hem of her dress. Her dark hair, plaited in a thick braid, reached the small of her back, but her face was still rosy and unlined. In truth, she couldn't have been more than a couple years older than the young bachelors of the village, but after being unmarried for seven years, they'd long since looked away.

She glanced down at her dress and smoothed out the wrinkles, then picked up her mother's quilt again, gazing at it wistfully. It just felt right to bring it out again and let it see the light. It was meant to be used. Before she could second-guess herself, Ingrid picked up the quilt, shut the lid of the chest, and marched out the door with her picnic basket on her arm and her dog Otto at her heels.

They followed the winding path out of the forest and into the village until they reached the meadow where a colorful spread of quilts and wildflowers dotted the clearing. There was a large pile of firewood, just waiting to be ignited at dusk, in the center of it all. The atmosphere was humming with cheerful voices, chirping birds, and the sound of trees being felled in the distance. Ingrid caught a side conversation as she passed a group of men stacking firewood. "I heard today's the day that Sven's boys will begin to look for their brides." Ingrid turned her head reflexively to listen. That was often part of the celebration. Unmarried men, who hadn't shown much initiative yet, went to the edge of the clearing and felled a tree, which was meant to show them the direction they should look to find a wife. It was an old tradition, not taken seriously by most. It did give the young men a chance to show off for the girls of the village, however, which they didn't seem to mind at all.

The festivities began and Ingrid settled down on her quilt with Otto close by. He licked her hand, begging for scraps, and she tossed him a breadcrust. Sven Hansson clapped his hands loudly and called out for everyone to hear, "As you all know, my two sons, Karl and Gustav, are now old enough to be called men." He winked and a few laughs echoed throughout the crowd. He continued, "The time has come for them to start looking for their brides!" He pointed to Karl, gesturing for him to go first. Karl walked purposefully out to the edge of the meadow and took up his axe, shearing down a young birch in no time. It fell to the south, in the direction of most of the cottages in the village, and he held up his hands in victory. The girls cheered especially loud for Karl. He was the oldest of Sven's sons, and although he was past the typical marrying age, he was handsome and well-liked. It would not be difficult for him to find a willing bride. Then it was Gustav's turn. He was a few years younger, tall and lean, with bright red hair that curled out from under the edges of his knit cap. His short beard was also red. He looked a bit sheepish as he took the axe from Karl's hands and went off in the opposite direction. Pausing at the edge of the trees, he was unsure about which one to choose and finally settled on a slim pine with scraggly branches. When he hefted the axe, however, it was clear that he was just as skilled as his brother. After a few earnest chops, the trunk cracked and Gustav jumped out of the way as the tree fell in an unexpected direction. There was an audible gasp. It had not fallen in the direction of the village at all. It pointed off toward the forest, where Ingrid's lone cabin stood.

As Ingrid watched the events unfold, she gripped the edges of her mother's quilt and pulled it up to her chin, as if to hide behind it. Heads began to turn in her direction. Otto's ears perked up at the attention and he nosed her hand for another treat. She froze for a split second and then quickly gathered up her picnic basket and took off running toward the forest with Otto leading the way, his tongue lolling out of his mouth and ears flapping in the wind. It was all a game to him and he was determined to get home first.

Ingrid reached the door a full minute after Otto, gasping for breath. She quickly opened the latch and hurried inside, locking it again, as if they were being pursued. Peeking out of the curtains, she slowed her breath and saw that no one had followed. The villagers would still be at the meadow, celebrating and singing together. She couldn't bring herself to return tonight and show her face. It was all too much to bear. The scrutiny and embarrassment turned her cheeks red at that instant and she sat in her rocker with her face in her hands. There was no chance a young man like Gustav would be interested in someone like her. He would be the laughingstock of the village if he ever came knocking at her cabin door. Another feeling rose up, unbidden, and she realized that she still wished he might.

Otto whined and paced at the door, wishing for another chase, and Ingrid bent down to run her fingers through his thick white fur. He licked her cheek and caught a tear that had escaped from the corner of her eye. Looking over at her cedar chest, Ingrid's heart suddenly sank. She'd forgotten her quilt back in the meadow. Either she would have to return and face everyone, or she'd have to wait until morning and go back for it, hoping it was still there and in one piece. She paced, wondering what to do, clutching at her chest and starting to cry again.

In the midst of Ingrid's worry and frustration, a soft knock at the door startled her. Otto barked and sniffed at the threshold. Ingrid quickly wiped tears from her cheeks and peeked through the window. It was Gustav. And he had her mother's quilt tucked under his arm.

to be continued...

Pinwheel block

BLOCK SIZE
8" Finished

SUPPLY LIST
(2) 10" white squares
(2) 10" blue squares

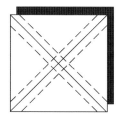

1 draw, layer and sew
Draw a line from corner to corner twice on the diagonal on the reverse side of each white square. Place a white square atop a blue square with right sides facing. Sew ¼" on either side of each of the drawn lines.

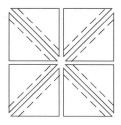

2 cut
Cut the sewn squares in half vertically and horizontally. Then cut on the drawn lines. Each set of sewn squares will yield 8 half-square triangles. A total of 16 are needed.

3 press and trim
Open each section to reveal a half-square triangle. Press the seam allowance toward the darker fabric. Trim each so it measures 4½".

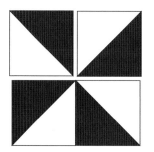

4 block construction
Lay out 4 half-square triangles. Sew 2 together into a row. Make 2 rows. Sew the rows together to complete the block.

Make 4 blocks.

broken orange peel

QUILT SIZE
59" X 67½"

QUILT TOP
2 packages 5" print squares
2¼ yards background fabric

OUTER BORDER
1¾ yards – includes fabric for
 sashing strips

BINDING
¾ yard

BACKING
3¾ yards – horizontal seam(s)

ADDITIONAL SUPPLIES
Glue Stick
Small Orange Peel Template

SAMPLE QUILT
Sundance by Sue Daley for
 Riley Blake

ONLINE TUTORIALS
msqc.co/blockwinter17

QUILTING
Loops and Swirls

PATTERN
pg. 8

checkered dresden

QUILT SIZE
79½" X 79½"

QUILT TOP
1 roll of 2½" strips
5¾ yards background fabric

OUTER BORDER
2 yards print – includes yardage to
    make circles for block centers

BINDING
¾ yard

BACKING
7½ yards – vertical seam(s)

ADDITIONAL SUPPLIES
MSQC Dresden Plate Template
½ yard lightweight fusible
    interfacing – We used Heat
    N Bond Feather Lite

SAMPLE QUILT
Artisan Batiks Daisy's Garden 3
    by Lunn Studios for Robert
    Kaufman

ONLINE TUTORIALS
msqc.co/blockwinter17

QUILTING
Flower Swirls

PATTERN
pg. 16

disappearing pinwheel arrow

QUILT SIZE
81" X 92"

QUILT TOP
1 package 10" print squares
1 package of 10" background
   squares

INNER BORDER
¾ yard

OUTER BORDER
1¾ yards

BINDING
¾ yard

BACKING
7½ yards – horizontal seam(s)

SAMPLE QUILT
Jubilee by Melody Miller for
   Cotton + Steel

ONLINE TUTORIALS
msqc.co/blockwinter17

QUILTING
Simply Roses

PATTERN
pg. 24

double
the fun

QUILT SIZE
89¾" x 102⅞"

QUILT TOP
1 package 10" print squares
2 yards light background fabric
2 yards dark background fabric

BORDER
1¾ yards

BINDING
1 yard

BACKING
8¼ yards - horizontal seam(s)

SAMPLE QUILT
Soleil by Whistler Studios
   for Windham Fabric

ONLINE TUTORIALS
msqc.co/blockwinter7

QUILTING
Loops and Swirls

PATTERN
pg. 32

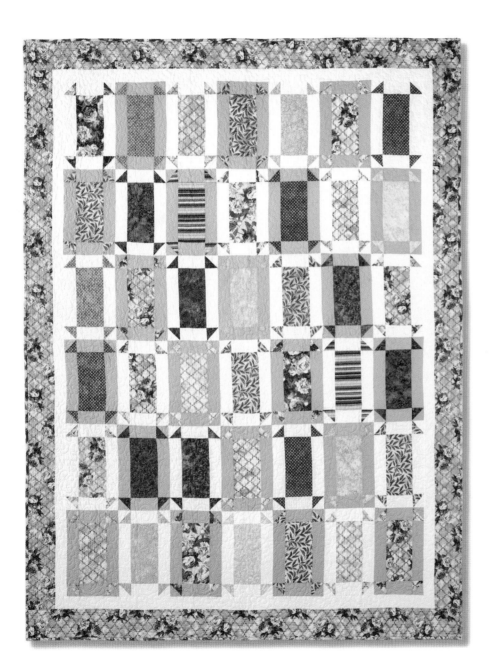

long shoofly

QUILT SIZE
72½" X 94"

QUILT TOP
1 package 10" squares
2¼ yards light solid background
  fabric - includes inner border
1¾ yards medium solid
  background fabric

OUTER BORDER
1¼ yards

BINDING
¾ yard

BACKING
5¾ yards - vertical seam(s)
  using 42" width of fabric

SAMPLE QUILT
Peony Passion by Linnea Washburn
for Northcott Fabrics

ONLINE TUTORIALS
msqc.co/blockwinter17

QUILTING
Curly Twirly Flowers

QUILT PATTERN
pg. 40

mini
tumbler

QUILT SIZE
20" X 40½"

QUILT TOP
2 packages – 42 ct. 2½" print
 squares *or* 1 package
 5" print squares
½ yard background fabric

BORDER
½ yard

BINDING
¼ yard

BACKING
1½ yards

ADDITIONAL SUPPLIES
MSQC Mini Tumbler Template

SAMPLE QUILT
Black and White by Jennifer
 Sampou for Robert Kaufman

ONLINE TUTORIALS
msqc.co/blockwinter17

QUILTING
Meander

QUILT PATTERN
pg.48

periwinkle

QUILT SIZE
58" X 70"

QUILT TOP
2 packages 5" print squares
3¾ yards background fabric

BORDER
1 yard

BINDING
¾ yard

BACKING
3¾ yards - horizontal seam(s)

ADDITIONAL SUPPLIES
1 package MSQC Wacky Web
    Triangle Papers
1 MSQC Small Periwinkle Template
    for 5" squares
Glue Stick - optional

SAMPLE QUILT
On Trend by Jen Allyson for
    Riley Blake

ONLINE TUTORIALS
msqc.co/blockwinter17

QUILTING
Forget me not

PATTERN
pg. 56

cornered drunkard's path

QUILT SIZE
64" X 73"

QUILT TOP
2¾ yards solid
5 yards background–
   includes outer border

BINDING
¾ yard

BACKING
4 yards (42" wide) – horizontal
   seam(s)

ADDITIONAL SUPPLIES
3 yards 24" Wide Fusible Interfacing
   (We used Steam-a-Seam 2 Lite)
Easy Circle Cut Ruler

SAMPLE QUILT
Cotton Supreme Solids - Redwork,
Optical White by RJR Fabrics

ONLINE TUTORIALS
msqc.co/blockwinter17

QUILTING
Curly Twirly Flowers

PATTERN
pg. 64